Antler

Henry Raith

Animals with Antlers

All of these animals have **antlers**.
Antlers are bones that grow out of an animal's head.
Most male deer, elk, and moose grow a new pair of antlers each year.

These animals are all members of the deer family.

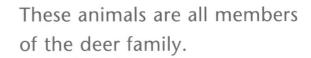

White-tailed deer

Elk

Moose

3

The antlers on these animals look different.
Their antlers are different sizes and shapes.
Their antlers have different numbers of sharp points.
These sharp points are called **tines**.

Which animal has the most tines on its antlers?

4

White-tailed deer

Moose

Elk

5

All antlers look like small bumps when they first **sprout**. The antlers grow quickly and begin to branch out. As antlers grow, they are covered with a soft layer of skin and hair called **velvet**.

Moose and elk antlers grow about **one inch** a day. Deer antlers grow about **one half inch** a day.

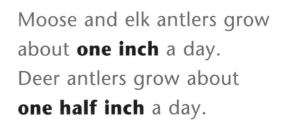

6

Elk

White-tailed deer

Moose

After a few months the antlers stop growing.
The velvet dries up and the animal rubs it off
on trees or shrubs.
Now the antlers are hard.
The animal carries the antlers for a few more months.
Then they fall off.

Elk antlers begin growing in
March. Elk have antlers for
9 or 10 months.

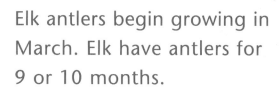

Elk

Deer Antlers

A deer's antlers grow up and out from its head.
Most white-tailed deer grow eight or ten tines
on their antlers.
Some white-tailed deer grow as many as 16 tines.

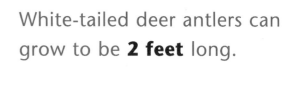

White-tailed deer antlers can
grow to be **2 feet** long.

Elk Antlers

An elk has larger antlers than a deer.
These antlers grow up and back from the top of
the elk's head.
Elk antlers usually have more tines than deer antlers.

Elk antlers can grow to be
4 feet long.

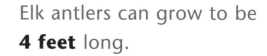

Moose Antlers

A moose's antlers grow out from the sides
of its head.
These antlers are flat in the center.
Moose grow the largest antlers of all!

A moose's antlers can weigh
60 pounds.

Glossary

antler a bone that grows out of an animal's head

sprout to begin to grow

tine a sharp point on an antler

velvet a soft layer of skin and hair on an antler